# HOW TO LEARN FRENCH IN CANADA

T0349902

❖ *How to Learn*

# French in Canada

## A HANDBOOK FOR
## ENGLISH CANADIANS

*Victor E. Graham*

UNIVERSITY OF TORONTO PRESS

© University of Toronto Press 1965
Reprinted 2017
ISBN 978-1-4875-9916-4 (paper)

# Preface

SOME OF THE PROBLEMS of creating and maintaining a genuinely bilingual and bicultural society are now clear to us. What is equally clear is that in identifying the problems, however satisfying an exercise that is, we do not thereby solve them. What such identification has indicated is that these problems have many facets: some are differences of opinion, some are matters of expectation, some matters of ignorance, some of unfulfilled hopes and intentions. It is largely to the latter that this book is addressed.

What is particularly evident is that whatever solutions do present themselves, many are matters of small but vital changes in our lives. They are, in short, matters that involve patience and a great deal of long-term effort. Despite some random hopes, the task is not going to be accomplished by acts of parliament or grand endeavour, but over a long period of time and slowly.

It is immediately apparent that the combination of the concern for bilingualism and biculturalism, or for language and culture, is a sensible and necessary one. To speak practically of grasping a culture, one must grapple with the primary thing—language. To encounter the learning of a language one cannot escape the cultural reinforcements that make its command and use plausible. Nor should one want to; it's not much fun without them. It is a dismally familiar refrain in many parts of Canada that an exposure to French, no matter how well disciplined and lengthy, is of little value unless there is a constant need to use it. And there is merit in the observation. Indeed the accumulated student-years of high school exposure to French that seem to have resulted only in an embarrassed fumbling with the rudiments appear to bear some unhappy witness to this fact. Equally convincing is the fact that so many of our French-speaking countrymen are bilingual, because there has been some functional reason for them to be so.

There are, so far as we can tell, many, many English-speaking Canadians who would like to be more proficient, reasonably proficient, in French. For many the living contact with French Canada is difficult and woefully limited. The ideal solution would be to make sure that a living French culture was spread evenly all across Canada; but until that is a reality, we shall have to make use of what cultural supports there are.

The essential premise of this book is that these supports are much greater than is commonly supposed. Our intention has been not only to make the learning and use of the language more intelligible, but also to provide a wide range of practical opportunities for contact and reinforcement through publications, radio, and association activities of a recognizable kind. Great credit is due the tireless and remarkable efforts of Professor Graham, the imaginative support of the Citizenship Branch of the Department of Citizenship and Immigration, and the confidence of the University of Toronto Press. We are pleased to be in their company.

The book itself will not solve the problem. Only the

efforts and determined curiosity of individual English Canadians will do that. For them the book has been created.

Alan M. Thomas,
Director, CAAE

*Toronto, 1965*

# Contents

# HOW TO LEARN FRENCH IN CANADA

# Introduction

THIS BOOK is intended for English-speaking Canadians who want to do something about learning French. It may be a question of starting from scratch or of reviving some almost-forgotten elements acquired in school a number of years ago. In either case, it is hoped that this manual will provide useful suggestions as to how to go about becoming fluent in French. What is offered here is not a course of instruction, but a listing of practical ways of applying oneself to a study of the language.

Presumably there is no need to convince most people of the value of learning French. There are business and cultural reasons for doing so, of course, but, more than anything else in Canada today, the paramount need is for all of us to be able to understand each other. The function of language is to communicate ideas, and only when we speak the same language as others are we really able to understand their problems and to make known our own thoughts and wishes. Language and culture are inextricably woven together, and a comprehension of one without the other is impossible. Through an improved knowledge of French Canada English-speaking Canadians stand to gain an appreciation and understanding of a different point of view, another system of logical reasoning, and another texture of civilization. Even where this insight does not lead to acceptance or agreement, it at least gives us the knowledge necessary for an appreciation of the other culture and its members.

At this stage it is no consolation to say that the ideal time to acquire languages is between the ages of four and ten. In recent years Dr. Wilder Penfield, the eminent Montreal neurosurgeon, has given vigorous support to the concept of introducing foreign languages into the elementary school. Dr. Penfield, one of the world's outstanding authorities on the physiology of the brain, has repeatedly said that the capacities of the brain change with age and that the time to begin foreign language studies is during early childhood.

The ideal method for learning a foreign language is, of course, to be placed in an environment in which that language alone is spoken. Dr. Penfield, on the basis of experience with his own family, believes that children who have had concentrated training during the crucial years can stop using the language for a time, if necessary, and then pick it up later in high school without much loss as far as accent is concerned.

For most of us, it is too late to profit from this advice, but we can at least agitate to have French taught in the elementary schools in our local communities for the benefit of our children. There are practical difficulties in the way of finding teachers, arranging time-tables, and so forth, but more and more school boards all across the country are introducing French into the elementary programme.

For the adult who wishes to study French, the approach is necessarily different, but the methods currently in vogue are a far cry from those in use twenty years ago. French is no longer taught as an academic exercise in conjugating verbs, parsing sentences, and translating excerpts from classical literature. Instead, the emphasis is on the spoken language, and the approved learning sequence is: hear, say, read, write. In order to counteract the disadvantage of maturity and analytical habits of mind, the adult student must be exposed to as much French as possible—*language saturation* is the term employed. An hour of casual study once a week will not produce very startling results!

Language learning is rarely effective when carried on independently. It is quite possible to learn subjects such as history, botany, or cost accounting on one's own, since each consists of an organized body of knowledge which can be mastered with patience and application. Language, however, is an elusive thing, not subject to the same sort of rules as these subjects, and the only satisfactory way to acquire it is with the guidance of an experienced teacher who can point out mistakes and keep the student on the right track.

Wherever possible, students of French are urged to enroll in courses offered in their own community. Suggestions about such courses are to be found in several sections of this book. For those in remote areas, or for those interested in supplementing such courses, various other possibilities are listed under such headings as "Records and Tapes," "Films," and "Radio and Television." Generally speaking, the average adult is not aware of the great variety of ways in which he can expose himself to French if he wishes to.

The basic principle in acquiring French is to hear the language as much as possible and to speak it at every opportunity. Here modesty is no virtue. One should forget about perfectionism and cultivate spontaneity.

Only by talking can one learn to communicate. All accents are not the same, any more than educational backgrounds, and one must learn to speak with a great variety of people on all sorts of topics.

This inevitably raises the old question about whether, in predominantly English-speaking parts of Canada, it is desirable to teach so-called Parisian French or Canadian French. In this connection, there is much confusion on the part of the uninformed public—confusion which is propagated by the conflicting comments of teachers and visiting Frenchmen.

The French spoken in Canada, let it be said, is just as "correct" compared with the French spoken in Paris as is the English in this country compared with that in London. There is a different accent, it is true, and there are some differences in meaning, especially in technical vocabulary, but this is equally true of Canadian and British English. One can cite shocking examples of uneducated speech in all centres, but then, no one would recommend as a model the language of a Montreal cab driver any more than that of an Alberta cowboy or a London dock worker. Impeccable standard French can be taught, and is being taught, by all well-educated French teachers, whether they are French-Canadian or European-French.

At the present time, it so happens that almost all the tried and tested teaching aids have been produced in France or in the United States by firms who have turned for technical assistance to French citizens living abroad. The history of language instruction in France goes back a long way, and only very recently has French Canada started to produce its own teaching aids. We now have a dictionary of Canadian French and Canadian English, instructional records of French-Canadian folk-songs, and

French-Canadian films and educational television, but there are still no distinctively French-Canadian record courses, few texts or periodicals (aside from newspapers), and little in the way of aids for those wishing to apply themselves directly to a study of the French-Canadian language. The reasons are not hard to find. Even the French-Canadian universities tend to use such programmes as the *Voix et images* method developed at St. Cloud when offering language courses in French to English-speaking Canadians. They may revise the programme, or adapt it to Canadian use, but it is basically the method developed in France. It is, then, just as impossible to distinguish between the purely French and French Canadian as it would be to isolate the purely English Canadian from British or American.

The term "English Canadian" sounds strange to our ears, even though we use "French Canadian" constantly. This will help us to understand why the French Canadians call themselves *Canadiens* and refer to English-speaking Canadians as *les Anglais*. They mean, of course, *les Canadiens anglais*, and this is just one small point of friction which tends to disappear when one begins to study the language. Many French Canadians (if you will pardon the expression) also insist on calling British Columbia *la Colombie canadienne*. The appellation "British" seems to them a misnomer, particularly when translated into French. When we stop to examine their reasoning, we can at least appreciate a logic which perhaps never occurred to us before.

All of which brings us back to the question of culture as it is inextricably bound up with the study of language. Anyone really interested in learning French must be ready to expose himself to as many facets of experience in French as possible. There is no quick and easy way to pick up a language, but one can make maximum progress through maximum exposure. If one begins with records, radio, television, and films, one can profitably go on to read periodicals, newspapers, and books. Membership in a French organization and contacts with French groups of all kinds can provide many opportunities to practise the language, and this is fundamental.

It is a mistake to assume that the same method would be equally satisfactory for every learner. Background and local conditions will differ vastly but in the following pages there are suggestions which should prove useful to every student of French regardless of his level of attainment. Readers may wish to use these suggestions separately or simultaneously. The list is by no means exhaustive, but it gives enough leads that any area of interest may be cultivated indefinitely.

# Quebec Government Services

WITHIN THE PROVINCE OF QUEBEC cultural activities come under the general direction of the *Ministère des affaires culturelles*. In this large and important government department there are many sections co-ordinating activities in the arts, publications, scholarships, and so forth. For general information or for specific information concerning a special interest, readers who write directly to the ministry in Quebec City can be assured of receiving a helpful reply.

There are, of course, a great many agencies in the province which are concerned with such matters as making and distributing films, publishing and selling books, fostering handicrafts, recording folk songs, and encouraging young artists and writers. The *Ministère des affaires culturelles* has information which it will send out on request on these and many other activities.

Another useful address for general inquiries is that of the French-Canadian equivalent of the Canadian Association for Adult Education. It is

L'Institut Canadien de l'Éducation des Adultes
3425, rue St. Denis
Montréal 18, P.Q.

# French Government Services

THE GOVERNMENT OF FRANCE has always taken a great interest in cultural affairs, and French embassies and consulates throughout the world are centres of information about education, scholarships, records, films and so forth. A letter addressed to the Cultural Attaché will assuredly receive a prompt, courteous, and helpful reply.

In Canada, the French Embassy is located at 42 Sussex Drive, Ottawa. Through its Information Services, there is available all kinds of documentation of a general nature about France and its overseas territories. There is also a Question and Answer Service. From Cultural Services one may obtain information about French educational institutions, summer schools, scholarships for study abroad, and so on. This department also administers a large library of 16 mm. films and records which may be borrowed without any charge except postage. (Catalogues may be obtained on request.)

Posters and tourist documentation are available at the French Government Tourist Office, 1170 Drummond Street, Montreal, and at the French National Railways Office, 1500 Stanley Street, Montreal.

In addition to the French Embassy in Ottawa, there are various consulates across the country which provide supplementary services. Generally speaking, these do not have films or records available, but they have some literature and can provide very helpful information about France, and about local French nationals and groups interested in French culture. They often also have lists of private teachers of French. The following addresses may prove useful for regional inquiries:

ALBERTA
Consulat de France
10038, 110ème Rue
Edmonton, Alta.

BRITISH COLUMBIA
Consulat Général de France
736 Granville Street
Vancouver, B.C.

MANITOBA
Consulat de France
40 Westgate
Winnipeg, Man.

NEW BRUNSWICK
Consulat de France
34 Williams Street
Moncton, N.B.

NOVA SCOTIA
Consulat de France
63 Victoria Road
Halifax, N.S.

ONTARIO
Consulat Général de France
185 Bay Street
Toronto, Ont.

QUEBEC

Consulat Général de France
1980 ouest, rue Sherbrooke
Montréal, P.Q.

Consulat Général de France
1445, avenue de la Tour
Québec, P.Q.

# French Clubs

## ALLIANCE FRANÇAISE DU CANADA

THE SINGLE MOST IMPORTANT organization fostering the French language and French culture in Canada is the *Alliance française*. This society, with headquarters in Paris, has affiliated branches throughout the world. In Canada, the National Secretary is Professor Jean Houpert of the University of Montreal, and at the present time there are twenty-three centres across the country. Activities include lectures in French, concerts, films, plays, and, very often, group instruction at various levels.

The *Alliance française* is entirely non-political and non-profit making. Annual membership fees range from $5 to $10 and they are used exclusively to meet local operating expenses. None of the money collected goes to the world centre in Paris, which nonetheless assists the Canadian organization in different ways. Each year it sponsors at least two prominent lecturers from France who cross Canada from coast to coast. In addition, each centre receives a monthly parcel of half a dozen recent books. Some centres have set up small lending libraries for their members, and others deposit these books in the local public library.

Membership in the *Alliance française* is open to all interested persons. It is not limited in any way, and it usually includes French nationals, French Canadians, Europeans whose second tongue is French, and all those English-speaking Canadians who are interested in improving or maintaining their French.

Recently, two new centres have been set up,—one in Regina and one in the Okanagan Valley. There is no limit to the number of centres that can be established, and such groups may participate in all national activities and call on either the Canadian secretary or the world secretary for advice and assistance.

Following is a list of *Alliance française* centres across Canada. The person named is the president (unless indicated otherwise), and one may be sure that an inquiry will be answered or passed on to the proper person even if the officers change.

BAIE COMEAU, P.Q.
Mme Gilles Rouleau
Baie Comeau

CALGARY, ALTA.
Dr. G. Collet
56 Holly Street
Calgary

EDMONTON, ALTA.
Mme Stéphanie Piaumier (Secretary)
10530 125th Street
Edmonton

HALIFAX, N.S.
M. Burns Adams (Secretary)
43 Larch Street
Halifax

HAMILTON, ONT.
  Mme A. S. Britton
  561 Cannon Street East
  Hamilton

KINGSTON, ONT.
  M. Léandre Bergeron
  Royal Military College
  Kingston

KITCHENER, ONT.
  Mme Jacqueline Camp
  553 Stirling Avenue North
  Kitchener

LONDON, ONT.
  Dr. R. W. Torrens, Department of French
  University of Western Ontario
  London

MONCTON, N.B.
  Révérend Père Daigle
  Université Saint-Joseph
  Moncton

MONTREAL, P.Q.
  M. Jean-Raymond Boudou (Secretary)
  5607, avenue Darlington
  Montréal 26

OKANAGAN DU SUD, B.C.
  M. Roger Michel
  374 Haynes Street
  Penticton

OTTAWA, ONT.
  M. Roger Duhamel
  Imprimeur de la Reine
  Ottawa

QUEBEC, P.Q.
M. Henri Beaupré
37, rue Sainte-Angèle
Québec

REGINA, SASK.
M. Charles Fresco
2542 McTavish
Regina

RIMOUSKI, P.Q.
M. Jacques Brillant
Rimouski

RIVIÈRE-DU-LOUP, P.Q.
Mme Lucien Bédard
2, rue de la Cour
Rivière-du-loup

SAINT-GEORGES DE BEAUCE, P.Q.
M. Jacques Pinon (Secretary)
Case postale 871
Saint-Georges de Beauce

SAINT-HYACINTHE, P.Q.
M. Jules Laframboise (Secretary)
2290, rue Beauparlant
Saint-Hyacinthe

SHERBROOKE, P.Q.
Mme Léonidas Bachand
6 sud, rue Wellington
Sherbrooke

TORONTO, ONT.
Professor C. E. Rathé
Victoria College, University of Toronto
Toronto

VANCOUVER, B.C.
M. Charles Bloch-Bauer
9252 Hudson Street
Vancouver 14

VICTORIA, B.C.
Mrs. K. D. Stone
1573 Wilmot Place
Victoria

WINNIPEG, MAN.
Mrs. Meredith Jones
347 Niagara Street
Winnipeg

## FRANCE–CANADA

This organization actually originated in Toronto in 1948. Two years later a number of groups in France which had as their main objective friendly relations with Canada chose exactly the same name by chance. *France–Canada* in Europe now exchanges information and visits with the Canadian centres, which have been extended to Montreal and Quebec, but the two are entirely independent.

*France–Canada* is mainly interested in social activities of various kinds. It aims to bring together French nationals and Canadians interested in the French language and French culture. Films, plays, banquets, and wine-tasting parties are all occasions for convivial gatherings where French alone is spoken. *France–Canada* also runs evening classes in Toronto for those wishing to learn French and it frequently organizes tours in Quebec and France and receives in this country members of the French branches who come here on visits.

For further information in the centres concerned, the following addresses may prove useful:

ONTARIO
Association France–Canada
P.O. Box 195
Terminal "A"
Toronto 1

QUEBEC
Mme A. D. Archambault
460, boulevard Lasalle
Verdun

Mlle Hélène Vrazian
167, avenue Saint Cyrille
Québec

## ALLIANCE CANADIENNE

This organization, as its name implies, has as its principal aim to foster friendly relations between French-speaking and English-speaking Canadians. Its activities are cultural and social, and the annual membership fee is around $5.00 for individuals, with special rates for couples and students.

Following is a list of centres where branches exist. The person named in each case is the president (unless otherwise indicated).

HAMILTON, ONT.
Mme James Currier (Secretary)
68 Prince George Avenue
Hamilton

MONTREAL, P.Q.
> M. A. Larocque
> 836 McEachen
> Outremont

OTTAWA, ONT.
> Major C. C. G. Bond
> 11 Fair Haven Way
> Ottawa 7

PORT ARTHUR, ONT.
> Mme Marie Brunnen (Secretary)
> 10, rue Algoma
> Port Arthur

QUEBEC, P.Q.
> M. Martial Roy (Secretary)
> 1396, rue Rousseau
> Sillery, P.Q.

SUDBURY, ONT.
> M. Fernand Morisset
> 181, avenue D'Youville
> Sudbury

TORONTO, ONT.
> Mme Gérard Godin
> 34 North Sherbourne
> Toronto 5

# Instruction Privately
# and in Groups

WITH THE RIGHT TEACHER, private tutoring in French is undoubtedly the best way to make rapid progress without any wasted efforts. The only trouble is that thoroughly competent instructors are hard to find. It is not enough to be French or to have a good educational background; one must also have experience and an understanding of the difficulties facing an English person learning the language. To put it another way, how many readers of this book would feel qualified to teach the elements of English to someone beginning the language?

The first word of caution, then, concerns the teacher. The second concerns the cost. Private lessons inevitably are much more expensive than group instruction. It is only natural that an experienced and successful tutor should be paid at a rate comparable to that which applies in the teaching of music, elocution, or of any other art. Fees normally range between $3 to $5 per hour. Lists of tutors are sometimes available through French Departments at universities, colleges and secondary schools, Boards of Education, local French organizations (*Alliance française, France–Canada*), French consulates, and so forth.

For most prospective students of French, group

instruction is entirely satisfactory and it costs a good deal less than private lessons. It has the advantage, too, of bringing together a number of people with the same interests. The teacher is likely to be well-trained and to have available a variety of audio-visual paraphernalia to which the private tutor would not necessarily have access.

Apart from universities and colleges, which are discussed elsewhere, most communities have a number of other organizations which offer instruction in French in the evenings. Almost all the large secondary school systems provide courses for adults in matriculation subjects. These usually meet once a week throughout the school year. They are very inexpensive, and even though they are oriented toward examinations, they can be followed with profit by anyone interested in the subject. A telephone call to the local Board of Education should provide the desired information, and in cases where no instruction is provided at present, a show of interest would no doubt lead to creation of a programme as it already has in other communities.

The Y.M.C.A. and the Y.W.C.A. frequently offer non-credit courses in French as part of their extension programme, as do the Y.M.H.A. and the Y.W.H.A. where these exist. The special work of the *Alliance française* and *France–Canada* is described in detail in another section. Where these organizations offer instruction in French, the level is always very high and the cost minimal. Other organizations which may offer courses in French include local Allied Arts or Arts Council centres and other similar cultural groups.

There are, of course, many commercial schools of language instruction. These go under the name of Linguists' Clubs, Academies of Languages, Schools of Languages, and so forth, and their standards vary tremendously.

Probably the best-known language school is Berlitz, which has centres in several Canadian cities. In effect, it employs private tutors to whom students are assigned for a programme to meet their individual needs. They are encouraged to have lessons as frequently as possible (every day, if they can) and the cost is correspondingly high. Berlitz is effective in a "blitz" programme for anyone who, perhaps for business reasons, must suddenly acquire the elements of a new language, but it is not the answer for the average individual who wants to learn French.

Some business firms anxious to have their employees learn French have incorporated a programme of instruction into regular office hours. A qualified teacher comes to the firm for an hour or so three or four times a week. This method provides the very best incentive because acquiring French is no longer a casual, extra-curricular affair but a highly-organized specific aim. With even a half-dozen or a dozen individuals involved, it is quite possible to obtain the services of a first-rate teacher and to orient the classes toward the particular aim in mind.

In order to find instruction in French, you may have to show unusual ingenuity. Telephone calls to the types of organizations mentioned, careful perusal of the yellow pages in the telephone directory, visits to local libraries, French restaurants, or French Catholic churches, even an advertisement in the local newspaper may be necessary before you find what you are looking for.

Private school systems, which may be used by groups under the direction of competent instructors, include the following:

*Je parle français,* distributed by the Encyclopaedia Britannica.

This course consists of 120 sound colour films, 120 tapes and texts with teacher's guide. The complete course may be purchased outright or in sections through an annual rental which can be applied to the total cost. This system is currently in use in Winnipeg in an evening Adult Education programme and results are said to be excellent. For further information, write to

Encyclopaedia Britannica
151 Bloor Street West
Toronto 5, Ontario

*Parlons français*, with Anne Slack.

This is a highly effective television series which may be shown locally by arrangement with Heath de Rochemont Corporation, 285 Columbus Avenue, Boston, Massachusetts 02116.

*Voix et images de France*

This method, which is described elsewhere (p. 54), is being used very widely in university extension programmes for adults who are beginning instruction. Those interested may enroll in a regular section or they may purchase the necessary equipment (filmstrips, tapes, teaching guide, textbooks) and hire their own teachers. The only word of caution concerns the instructor, since it is indispensable to have someone familiar with the method in order for it to be effective. Inquiries should be directed to one of the French bookstores in Montreal (see the partial list on p. 84).

# Records and Tapes

THE MOST POPULAR METHOD of studying languages now-adays is to purchase a series of records or tapes which may or may not be accompanied by printed material—copies of the texts used, exercises, vocabularies. Many of these systems have been highly advertized and would-be purchasers are often encouraged to believe that a few hours of recreational listening will produce fluency as if by magic. There is no "French without toil," except for children brought up in a French-speaking area, and results obtained in learning a language are directly pro-portionate to the time and the effort involved.

This is not to say that the record or tape method is not valuable. Many such systems have been in use for a long time and they have been constantly improved and up-dated by experts. The voices heard are in general the very best available anywhere. From one point of view it is true to say that a good record or tape system permits the student to introduce into his own living room the most highly-qualified private tutors to be found. How he responds to their tuition is a personal matter, and the only serious drawback is that they cannot correct him. This he must do for himself. For that reason, the record or tape method is most effective when it is supplemented by private or class instruction.

Some methods of record or tape instruction have been on the market for many years. The Cortina Academy claims that it is the oldest, but Linguaphone is probably a close second. The best known method in France is that developed by Assimil for foreigners wishing to learn the language. In the United States the method perfected for the instruction of army personnel during the Second World War is now marketed under the title *Living Language*.

It would be impossible either to list all the reputable language records in French or to recommend any one method which would suit the needs of all prospective learners. Many libraries have available one or more of the most popular series. The best idea is to listen to a few records first in order to determine whether they are too elementary or too advanced.

After the student has had some practice in hearing oral French, he may wish to buy some of the records which include specialized vocabulary or regional accents. Many records include both men's and women's voices and they provide excellent practice in listening to a variety of voices.

The following list is representative only. Where possible, the Canadian distributor has been indicated but there is no guarantee that all records are available locally. If stuck, try writing to either of the following:

> Wible Language Institute
> 24 South Eighth Street
> Allentown, Pennsylvania 18105
>
> Centrale audio-visuelle, inc.
> 260 ouest, rue Faillon
> Montréal 10

COMPLETE FRENCH LANGUAGE COURSES

*Cortina Language Course: French*
Fifteen 12-inch 78 r.p.m. records.
PRODUCER-DISTRIBUTOR:

Cortina Academy
136 West 52 Street
New York 19.

Voices are pleasing. Intonations, emphasis, and accent are all good. The records were originally intended for individual rather than group study and serve best for the purpose of studying alone.

An accompanying 400-page book contains the text of the lessons and conversations as well as a reference grammar. *Price*: $60 approx.

*Linguaphone*
Sixteen 10-inch 78 r.p.m. records; also available on 45 r.p.m. records or tapes.
PRODUCER-DISTRIBUTOR:

Linguaphone Institute
970 McEachran Avenue
Montreal 8, P.Q.

Complete kit includes an illustrated text of the recorded material, workbooks, and a manual of instructions. Voices and recording are excellent, content good standard French. Intended for self-teaching by mature students. *Price*: $60 approx.

*Le Français sans peine* (French Without Toil)
Twenty 10-inch 78 r.p.m. records, or five 12-inch 33⅓ r.p.m. records.
PRODUCER: Assimil (France). These records may be obtained through Montreal bookstores or La Librairie française, 39 Gerrard West, Toronto.

This series of recordings is intended for individual study. The variety of voices is good, as is the pronunciation, although the latter is occasionally somewhat artificial on the initial records because of the slow speed requirements for beginning comprehension. Intonations and accents are satisfactory. Voices of about 15 men and women. Accompanying text. *Price*: $50 approx.

*Funk and Wagnalls' Language Phone Method*
Six 12-inch 33⅓ r.p.m. records, or eighteen 10-inch 78 r.p.m. records.
PRODUCER-DISTRIBUTOR:

> Funk and Wagnalls
> 360 Lexington Avenue
> New York, N.Y. 10017

The records are accompanied by a manual of the material used, plus a self-teaching textbook. *Price*: $50 approx.

*New French Self-Taught*
Six 12-inch 33⅓ r.p.m. records or eighteen 10-inch 78 r.p.m. records.
A revision of a well-established self-taught system of language study with recordings by Professor Pierre Brodin of the Lycée français in New York and Eve Daniel of the French Art Theatre. *Price*: $55 approx.

*Spoken French*
Twenty-four 12-inch 78 r.p.m. records, or six 12-inch 33⅓ r.p.m. records.
DISTRIBUTOR:

> Holt, Rinehart and Winston
> 833 Oxford Street
> Toronto 18

These records, prepared by François Denoeu (Dartmouth) and R. A. Hall (Cornell), are accompanied by a text and a key to exercises and tests. The French is the colloquial, everyday speech of the better educated Parisian. Useful to individuals working alone or in small study groups. *Price*: $50 approx.

*Le Français chez vous*
 Five 12-inch 33⅓ r.p.m. records with text.
 Recorded by the R.T.F. (the French Government's broadcasting system) in Paris, this set was designed by a professor of French at the Sorbonne and the director of the Laboratory of Living Languages at the École Normale Supérieure de Saint-Cloud. Forty prominent French actors and singers were used to record the lessons, thereby assuring ideal pronunciation and intonation for the student to imitate. The lessons (52) are in the form of amusing playlets. Each lesson presents multiple voices in dialogue form. Each dialogue is constructed to illustrate and drill the structure of the language. Each lesson is followed by a multiple-voiced review and exercises, with pauses for imitation. The subject matter covers modern life in France. The modern, colloquial French is spoken by French people as nearly as possible in the circumstances of their everyday lives. Songs are introduced to illustrate points of lessons. The 260-page illustrated text published by Didier, Paris, contains all the recorded material plus additional exercises and questions and answers designed to fix in the student's mind the main points of the lesson. *Price*: $40 approx.

## INTRODUCTORY LANGUAGE COURSES
*Living Language: French*
 Four 10-inch 33⅓ r.p.m. records.

PRODUCER-DISTRIBUTOR:

Greystone Corporation
41 Bertal Road
Toronto 15, Ont.

These recordings are excellent. Pronunciation, intonations, and accent are all fine. The records are functional, the vocabulary basic and good. *Price*: $12 approx.

*Gateway to French*
Two 12-inch 33⅓ r.p.m. records.

PRODUCER-DISTRIBUTOR:

Ottenheimer Publishers
99 Painters Mill Road
Owings Mills, Maryland 21117

Records are accompanied by a Conversation Manual and a Phrase Index. Native speakers use conversational method of instruction. Good. *Price*: $12 approx.

*French Through Pictures*
Two 12-inch 33⅓ r.p.m. records.

PRODUCER-DISTRIBUTOR:

Educational Services
1730 Eye Street N.W.
Washington 6, D.C.

This method is an extension of the English Through Pictures concept developed by I. A. Richards, Christine Gibson, and Associates at Harvard University. The records parallel the first half of a Pocket Book text. There are also two workbooks available and, for those interested, a tape recording of the complete book (7½ or 3¾ ips.). Especially fine pronunciation, enunciation, and accent. Excellent for first instruction. Records, $10. Texts, $.45 each. Set of Six Tapes, $45.

*Language Familiarization Courses: French*
Two 12-inch 33⅓ r.p.m. records.
PRODUCER-DISTRIBUTOR:

> Educational Services
> 1730 Eye Street, N.W.
> Washington 6, D.C.

These records, produced for the United States Department of Defense, feature English interspersed with native French. There is an accompanying manual. *Price*: $5.95.

*Speak and Read French, Part I*
Three 12-inch 33⅓ r.p.m. records with text.
PRODUCER: Folkways Records
DISTRIBUTOR:

> Allied Record Corporation
> 5963 Monkland Avenue
> Montreal, P.Q.

Prepared and narrated by Professors Armand and Louise Bégué, these two records deal with grammatical points. *Price*: $20 approx.

*Speak and Read French, Part II*
Two 12-inch 33⅓ r.p.m. records with text.
PRODUCER: Folkways Records
DISTRIBUTOR:

> Allied Record Corporation
> 5963 Monkland Avenue
> Montreal, P.Q.

Conversational French prepared and read by Professors Armand and Louise Bégué. These records are designed to provide the student with a minimal practical vocabulary with which to carry on everyday conversation in idiomatic French. *Price*: $13.95.

*On parle français*
    Twelve 7-inch 33⅓ r.p.m. records.
    The records are supplemented by a manual containing the verbatim text of the recordings. Sixty-one lesson units are paced for beginner/intermediate practice. Native French male voices are heard in a large variety of monologues, dialogues, questions and answers, and folk songs. *Price*: $20.

*Basic Conversational French*
    Two 12-inch 33⅓ r.p.m. records with text.
    Julian Harris and André Leveque have prepared 41 conversations transcribed by a native French cast with pauses for the student. *Price*: $13 approx.

*Modern French by Sound*
    Available in 78, 45 or 33⅓ r.p.m. records at the same price ($8.50).
    PRODUCER-DISTRIBUTOR: RCA Victor
    This album of modern, contemporary French spoken by Professor and Mrs. Henri Peyre of Yale University is designed to give the student an expedient refresher course, a comprehensive foundation in pronunciation, and first-hand contact with practical, everyday, conversational French. An accompanying handbook includes lessons, grammar, exercises, and a vocabulary.

FRENCH LIFE AND TRAVEL
*La Famille Dubois*
    One 5-inch dual track reel at 7.5 ips, or one 3-inch dual track reel at 3.75 ips.
    PRODUCER-DISTRIBUTOR: EMC Recording Company
    Very interesting, practical material adapted to intermediate groups. An excellent variety of voices is offered. High production standards are maintained.

*La Vie française*

Five 5-inch dual track reels at 7.5 ips, or five 3-inch dual track reels at 3.75 ips.

PRODUCER-DISTRIBUTOR: EMC Recording Company

Conversations between an American girl and a French family comparing and contrasting French and American customs. Simple vocabulary.

1. Présentation de la famille
   Un Repas
   La petite Ville
   L'École primaire
   Le Lycée
   Le Bureau
2. Les Courses
   Le Marché
   Préparer la cuisine
   Visite du jour de l'an
   Écrire une lettre
   Maladie
3. Départ en vacances
   La Plage
   La Pêche
   Le Cinéma
   Le Scoutisme
   Garçons et filles
4. Au Café le dimanche
   Le 14 juillet
   Une Fête de sport, football
   Le Ski famille
   Le Tour de France
5. Une Pique-nique en vélo
   La Ferme
   La Campagne
   La Couturière

Le Bureau de tabac
Le Boulanger-pâtissier

*Listen and Learn French*
Three 10-inch 33⅓ r.p.m. records; 128-page manual, album.

DISTRIBUTOR: Dover Publications, Inc.

These recordings are designed specifically for the traveller. One and a half hours of speech contain 812 foreign phrases and sentences, each selected to fit a special situation. English sentences are given with French equivalents. *Price*: $5.95 per set.

*French Travel Course*
For the advanced student; 32 "guided tours" to places of cultural interest in France and Belgium; conversations on aspects of French geography, history, artistic heritage, political, economic, and social life; four speakers on the staff of the French National Radio. Course consists of an illustrated textbook and 16 records in a carrying case. *Price*: $50 approx.

*Spoken French for Students and Travellers*
Two 7-inch dual track reels at 7.5 ips, or two 5-inch dual track reels at 3.75 ips.

PRODUCER-DISTRIBUTOR: National Tape Library, University of Colorado, Boulder, Colorado

Recording of all text material in a 170-page book, giving much opportunity for oral and aural training. Excellent conversational material and a good variety of voices offered.

*Talking Your Way Through France*
Five 10-inch 78 r.p.m. records.

PRODUCER-DISTRIBUTOR: Cortina Academy

These recordings are primarily intended for home or

individual use. They attack the tourist's communication problems, as the title implies. Voices are good. Accents and intonations are excellent.

*Journey in French, Vol. I*

Nine separate Paris dialogue stories of a Frenchman and his wife with American friends; tours to Notre Dame cathedral, the Sorbonne, restaurants, shops, and discussions of food, architecture, history, education, sports, etc. Course consists of one 12-inch 33⅓ r.p.m. record and text. *Price*: $5.95.

*Journey in French, Vol. II*

Dialogue, spoken by native Frenchmen, covering travel, camping, post office, clothing, etc. Consists of one 12-inch 33⅓ r.p.m. record with 104-page text. *Price*: $7.95.

*Circling the Globe with Speech: French*

Three 12-inch 33⅓ r.p.m. records.

PRODUCER-DISTRIBUTOR: Wilmac Recorders

Useful both for training in aural comprehension and as a source of information concerning local culture and customs. The first record includes narrators from Dijon, Lorraine, Angers, the Latin Quarter, Paris, Saint-Gervais-les-Bains, Nice. The second record offers narrators from Wasquehal, Fille, Avignon, Orléans, Paris, Biarritz, Espelette, Marseilles. The third has a series of conversations between students about a variety of subjects including a description of a train trip; an initiation ceremony in an art school in Grenoble; a fishing adventure in the village of Conquet; student life in Paris. *Price*: $5.95 each.

*Promenades en France, I*

One 5-inch dual track reel at 7.5 ips, or one 3-inch dual track reel at 3.75 ips.

PRODUCER-DISTRIBUTOR: EMC Recording Company

A class tour involving famous sites of Paris. Useful for cultural values and comprehension.

*Contents*

Promenade à Paris
Au Restaurant
Soirée à Montmartre
Étudiant à Paris
Boul' Mich
Cité Universitaire
Les Bouquinistes par la Seine

*Promenades en France, II*

One 5-inch dual track reel at 7.5 ips, or one 3-inch dual track reel at 3.75 ips.

PRODUCER-DISTRIBUTOR: EMC Recording Company

A class tour involving well known sections of Brittany and the south of France. Useful for cultural values and comprehension.

*Contents*

La belle France
Châteaux de la Loire
Au Pays des coiffes (Bretagne)
La vieille France (vieille)
Mont Saint-Michel
Notre Dame de Chartres
Carcassonne

*Living and Working in France Series*

These tapes are extremely useful for gaining fluency in French. Various phases of society and culture are discussed in detail and each tape is supplemented with a manual. Prices vary from $1.50 to $6.50. The complete set of 23 types costs about $80.

DISTRIBUTOR:
Gaithersburg Photo and Audio-Visual Center
216 East Diamond Avenue
Gaithersburg, Maryland 20760

*Titles*

Les Saisons
Instruction en France
Professions en France
Commerce en France
Travaux à l'aiguille
A la campagne
Le Dîner est servi
Formules de conversation
La France: Administration et constitution
Distractions et passe-temps
Éléments d'arithmétique
Jours de fête
Temps, Date, Age
Maison, Pension, Hôtel
Santé et le corps humain
Je m'habille
La Famille
Monnaies, Poids, Mesures
Quel temps fait-il?
L'Heure et les horloges
Mon Tour de Paris
Magasins et achats
Visites et formules de politesse

# *Films*

IT IS ALWAYS INTERESTING to see French films when they are available in local theatres, but very often an English sound-track has been dubbed in or there are sub-titles in English. The sight of English on the screen completely destroys the effect of the French dialogue, and the beginning language student derives little benefit from this type of film.

Not many individuals have facilities for showing films in their homes, but there is certainly no better way to improve one's oral French while at the same time increasing one's acquaintance with French culture. Films introduce us to the country and the people and, unlike television programmes they can be shown over and over again. Usually they have a variety of voices, young and old, male and female, and a good cross-section of accents, urban and rural, Parisian and regional.

We are all aware of the tremendous range of accents in English, and most of us can distinguish them on fairly broad lines at least. We may not be able to analyse speech as skilfully as Professor Higgins in *Pygmalion/My Fair Lady*, but the more practice we have, the easier it becomes to recognize characteristic features which reveal background, education, and so forth.

The same thing is true for French, although the

foreigner can never hope to be able to analyse subtle distinctions in pronunciation. He will probably be satisfied if he can just understand a speaker whose accent differs from the norm! We all know how difficult it is to follow a Cockney, a Southerner, or a Liverpudlian, but a first encounter with such a person is not nearly as disturbing as meeting an individual who speaks a variety of French that is completely incomprehensible for someone who has already spent several years studying the language.

The only way to counteract this "traumatic" experience is to listen to as many voices as possible. Certain principles soon become evident. Women usually seem to be easier to understand than men because they speak more clearly and the pitch of their voices is higher. Similarly, older people are generally easier to follow because they tend to speak more slowly. Preachers, teachers, and radio announcers are trained in expressing themselves and they are more easily understood than cab drivers, waitresses, hairdressers, etc. However, the general impression that Frenchmen speak much more quickly than English speakers is quite false. This impression is derived from their vigorous articulation and the fact that the foreigner understands nothing or very little of what is being said.

Films have an advantage over radio or records in that one is able to see people speaking under natural conditions. It is sometimes useful to concentrate exclusively on sounds, but one must also associate voices with faces and learn to understand meanings from an added gesture, an incomplete sentence, a muttered aside. The film is an excellent introduction to real-life situations, and it is amazing what a variety is available at little or no cost. If individuals cannot show them in their own homes, groups can often make arrangements to rent a projector or meet at a church, school or club.

Generally speaking, most organizations which have French films to lend expect borrowers to pay only express charges, which will vary from $1 or $2 to $5, depending on the distance involved. In any case the amount is negligible, and many of the films are superb.

The following list indicates embassies, consulates, and other agencies which have 16 mm. French films available on these terms:

L'Ambassade de France
42 Sussex Drive
Ottawa, Ont.
(Catalogue of over 300 films available on request, most of them excellent but some rather old and of poor quality)

Services Officiels du Tourisme Français
1170 Drummond Street
Montreal, P.Q.
(Over 300 films available)

Consulate General of the Federal Republic of Germany
1501 McGregor Street
Montreal 25, P.Q.
(About 130 films available with commentary in French)

Cultural Service
USSR Embassy
285 Charlotte Street
Ottawa, Ont.
(About 50 films available with commentary in French)

Embassy of the Czechoslovak Socialist Republic
171 Clemow Avenue
Ottawa, Ont.
(Some 30 French language films available)

Royal Danish Embassy
446 Daly Avenue
Ottawa, Ont.
(A half-dozen films available with French
    commentary)

The Royal Embassy of Sweden
140 Wellington Street
Ottawa, Ont.
(A few films available with French commentary)

In addition, the Canadian Film Institute (1762 Carling Avenue, Ottawa 13) distributes films in French at a very low fee (25¢ to $3 per film) for the embassies of the United States, Great Britain, Australia, The Netherlands, and many other countries. The following film libraries act as agents for the Canadian Film Institute:

ALBERTA, SASKATCHEWAN, MANITOBA
    Supervisor of Adult Education
    University of Saskatchewan
    Saskatoon, Sask.

BRITISH COLUMBIA
    Supervisor, Audio-Visual Services
    Department of University Extension
    University of British Columbia
    Vancouver

NOVA SCOTIA, NEW BRUNSWICK, PRINCE EDWARD
ISLAND, NEWFOUNDLAND
    Audio-Visual Bureau
    Teachers' College
    Fredericton, N.B.

ONTARIO
Canadian Film Institute
1762 Carling Avenue
Ottawa

QUEBEC
Film Library
Macdonald College
Ste Anne de Bellevue

Different catalogues are available from the Canadian Film Institute on demand, and a partial list of French catalogue titles includes the following:

Orientation professionnelle
Développement des adolescents
Sports nautiques
Jeux de balles
Premiers secours
Groupe de Guides
Le Cinéma
Sports d'hiver
Préparation à la vieillesse
Grands moyens d'information

For more specific information, one should write to the Information Bureau of the Canadian Film Institute, 1762 Carling Avenue, Ottawa 13.

In 1963 the National Film Board added some 150 new 16 mm. films to an already considerable list of over 400 films with commentary or dialogue in French. These are available in local libraries, and for specific information concerning provincial centres, prospective borrowers should write to the regional office of the NFB.

ALBERTA, SASKATCHEWAN, MANITOBA
Suite 202, Federal Building
Saskatoon, Sask.

BRITISH COLUMBIA
> Suite 415, Federal Building
> 325 Granville Street
> Vancouver

NEW BRUNSWICK, NOVA SCOTIA, PRINCE EDWARD ISLAND
> New Federal Building
> (C.P. 216)
> Fredericton, N.B.

NEWFOUNDLAND
> Centre Building
> Church Hill (C.P. 1206)
> St. John's

ONTARIO
> Mackenzie Building
> 1 Lombard Street
> Toronto

QUEBEC
> 685, rue Cathcart
> (C.P. 998, Station B)
> Montréal

In certain cities there are very extensive collections of French language films in special libraries, but these are usually only available to local borrowers. Worth special mention are the following:

> Cinémathèque de la Bibliothèque Municipale
> de Montréal
> 2207 Montcalm Street
> Montreal 24, P.Q.

> Cinémathèque française du Manitoba
> Saint-Boniface, Man.

The Metropolitan Film Library
220 College Street
Toronto 2B, Ont.

Further information on local film libraries can usually be obtained either from the regional office of the National Film Board or from a special provincial council, if one exists in your province. For Quebec and Ontario, one should write to

L'Office du film de la province de Québec
Québec, P.Q.

and the

Ontario Association of Film Councils, Inc.
1 Lombard Street
Toronto, Ont.

# Radio and Television

IN ADDITION TO records and films, radio and television programmes in French should provide varied and interesting fare for those anxious to improve their knowledge of the language as quickly as possible. In this connection, we are all more or less at the mercy of our local stations, but it is surprising how much is available right across the country.

Television is, of course, more limited than radio, and at the present moment the only French language stations outside Quebec are Channel 10 in Cheticamp, N.S. (CBFCT), Channel 11 in Moncton, N.B. (CBAFT), Channel 10 in Saint-Quentin, N.B. (CHAU-TV-2), Channel 13 in Edmunston, N.B. (CJBR-TV-1), Channel 9 in Ottawa (CBOFT), Channel 13 in Sudbury, Ontario (CBFST-1), Channel 6 in Timmins, Ontario (CFCL-TV), Channel 3 in Kapuskasing, Ontario (CFCL-TV-1) and Channel 2 in Kearns, Ontario (CFCL-TV-2) (both rebroadcasting Timmins programmes), and Channel 6 in Winnipeg (CBWFT). In Edmonton, Channel 5 (CBXT) offers some regular French language programmes.

Occasionally French programmes are televised on the English network of the CBC. The only way to keep informed concerning these rare treats is to subscribe to the *CBC Times*, which costs $3 per year and is published weekly for the regions concerned. It includes listings for both television and radio:

LA SEMAINE À RADIO CANADA (FRENCH EDITION)
(Television: Montreal, Ottawa, Moncton, Winnipeg; Radio: Montreal, Quebec, Chicoutimi, Moncton, Toronto, Ottawa)
c/o Les Services d'Information
Société Radio Canada
C.P. 6000
Montréal, P.Q.

CBC TIMES, EASTERN EDITION
(Television and Radio for CBC stations in Ontario)
c/o Canadian Broadcasting Corporation
Box 5000
Toronto 1, Ont.

CBC TIMES, MARITIMES EDITION
(Television and Radio for Nova Scotia, New Brunswick, Prince Edward Island)
c/o Canadian Broadcasting Corporation
Box 5000
Toronto 1, Ont.

CBC TIMES, PRAIRIE EDITION
(Television and Radio for the Prairie Provinces plus Kenora)
c/o Canadian Broadcasting Corporation
Box 160
Winnipeg, Man.

CBC TIMES IN BRITISH COLUMBIA
(Television and Radio for British Columbia)
c/o Canadian Broadcasting Corporation
701 Hornby Street
Vancouver, B.C.

On the English radio network of the CBC there are
several regular bilingual programmes which have been
appearing for some years. Many readers will already be
familiar with the half hour of French which precedes the
broadcasts of the Metropolitan Opera on Saturday after-
noons. For the first fifteen minutes, the programme is
called *Time For French* with Gérard Arthur, and this is
followed by *Chansonnettes*, a selection of French songs
introduced by Jacques Desbaillets, one of Montreal's
best-known radio and television personalities.

Gérard Arthur has been with the CBC since the day
it started, almost thirty years ago on November 2, 1936.
He has served as the CBC's chief French announcer, as
assistant programme director for the Quebec Region,
and as the CBC's first French-language war correspondent. He writes his own material, which is mainly in the
form of dialogues with his wife, Sheila, an English Mon-
trealer. The informal sketches are devised in such a way
that listeners who understand little or no spoken French
will be able to follow what is going on. The husband and
wife team weave English and French into their dialogues,
sometimes translating, sometimes not.

Arthur is very frank about the nature of his refreshing
programme. "When you open your mouth to make
French noises," he says, "you're not going to sound, even
to yourself, like a Frenchman. Very few people acquire
such perfect bilingualism, and it is not possible without
exceptional gifts—and the opportunity to exploit them.
And most of us have neither. By listening to my French
you will hear how it is spoken by a moderately well-
educated male adult. Listening to my wife's will give you
an idea of what *you* may hope to sound like."

Another bilingual programme directed mainly toward

very young listeners is *Chez Hélène,* which appeared first on radio but which is now to be seen on television during day-time hours. On this programme the hostess is Hélène Baillargeon, the well-known folk-singer and entertainer from Montreal. She never speaks English, although she obviously understands the language. Other participants on this programme include a puppet mouse which speaks only English and youngsters who are learning French. The programme is intended for pre-school children but it is also watched with interest and profit by many mothers who take advantage of the opportunity to sit down with their four- and five-year olds.

There are also a number of school broadcasts available over the CBC. Information on National School broadcasts and telecasts can be obtained through the regional CBC Information Service. Popular and successful television programmes which may or may not be available locally are the series *En France comme si vous y étiez* with Dawn Addams and *Speaking French* with Professor Jean-Paul Vinay of the University of Montreal.

At the present time, the CBC in collaboration with Laval University and a number of other Canadian universities is preparing a programme of television instruction in French to be started in the fall of 1965. Under this programme, local teachers will be available to supplement television teaching and to mark and correct assignments.

In addition to the CBC and its affiliated stations, there are, of course, many radio stations in Canada outside the province of Quebec which broadcast partly or entirely in French. CBC affiliates include the French language stations in Winnipeg (St. Boniface), Saskatoon, Gravelbourg, and Edmonton. It is not possible to give a com-

plete list, but residents within the range of audibility of
the following stations may wish to see if they can get
them on their own sets.

| Location | Station | Frequency |
|---|---|---|
| Cornwall, Ont. | CFML | 1,100 |
| Edmonton, Alta. | CHFA | 680 |
| Edmunston, N.B. | CJEM | 570 |
| Gravelbourg, Sask. | CFGR | 1,230 (evening hours) |
| Gravelbourg, Sask. | CFRG | 710 (day-time hours) |
| Moncton, N.B. | CBAF | 1,300 |
| Ottawa, Ont. | CBOF(FM) | 1,250 |
| St. Boniface, Man. | CKSB | 1,050 |
| Saskatoon, Sask. | CFNS | 1,170 |
| Sudbury, Ont. | CFBR | 550 |
| Timmins, Ont. | CFCL | 620 |
| Toronto, Ont. | CJBC | 860 |

# Instruction by Correspondence

IT IS OBVIOUS that instruction by correspondence must concentrate on improving one's ability to write and read French, but it can be very useful if supplemented with oral practice of some sort. For individuals in isolated communities or for those whose commitments might prevent them from attending regular evening classes, a programme of correspondence instruction along with regular listening to records or tapes can work wonders.

The Department of Education of each provincial government maintains a Correspondence Branch which provides instruction for individuals not in attendance at regular school classes. The lessons are directed toward Junior and Senior Matriculation examinations because they are primarily intended for those who wish to obtain these certificates, but generally speaking there is no restriction on enrolment except the student's ability to profit from the instruction. In most provinces French is available from the Grade VIII (or IX) level through to Grade XII (or XIII). Exceptions here are Newfoundland, Quebec, and Prince Edward Island, which do not provide any instruction in the upper years.

In most provinces correspondence instruction is free to residents of the province, although some (e.g. Nova

Scotia) charge a small fee. An enquiry to the Correspondence Branch, in care of the Department of Education in the appropriate regional provincial capital should elicit the required information. In certain provinces (e.g. Newfoundland, Nova Scotia) correspondence instruction can be supplemented by radio or television programmes in French designed for school consumption. These are broadcast during regular school hours, of course, and therefore would only be useful to those able to tune in to them.

There are a very few universities which also provide instruction by correspondence. (The best known is perhaps Queen's University, Kingston, Ont.) Generally speaking this instruction is available only to high school graduates, and it is intended to lead to university credits. An exception is Mount Allison University (Sackville, N.B.) which has a wide programme of extra-mural courses open to anyone desiring to widen his intellectual horizons in the liberal arts, and no evidence of previous education is required from those who do not desire degree credit, and who do not intend, therefore, to write examinations. The programme includes a number of French courses.

# Universities

THOSE COMMUNITIES in which there is a university or a college of some sort are particularly fortunate when it comes to language instruction. In the first place, universities require highly-trained teachers and they tend to attract specialists, including those whose native language is French. It is not true that individuals whose native language is French always make the best teachers of French, but when they have had the necessary training they undoubtedly do. Moreover, universities tend to be interested in extension work, and they regard the offering of evening courses for interested adults as part of their responsibility.

University courses offered may be roughly divided into credit and non-credit courses. In order to enroll in the former, students must have the necessary entrance requirements, Senior Matriculation or its equivalent, and they must conform to university regulations concerning attendance, examinations, and so forth. Only under special circumstances will university authorities permit "occasional" students to audit courses from the regular degree programmes.

Generally speaking, no restrictions are imposed on students seeking to enroll in non-credit courses which are almost invariably offered in the evening from September or October through to late March or April. Sometimes only a limited number of students will be accepted in language classes (15 to 25), and for that reason it is wise to apply well in advance. Usually a registration fee of from $3 to $5 is required, and the tuition fees vary depending on the length of the course and the frequency of meetings.

Most non-credit courses in French meet once a week in the evening for an hour and a half or two hours. Such courses normally last twenty to thirty weeks, and the total fees vary from $25 to $45.

A partial list of universities offering such courses includes the following:

ALBERTA

    The University of Alberta, Edmonton
    The University of Alberta, Calgary
    Lethbridge Junior College, Lethbridge

BRITISH COLUMBIA

    The University of British Columbia, Vancouver
    Victoria University, Victoria

MANITOBA

    The University of Manitoba, Winnipeg
    United College, Winnipeg
    Brandon College, Brandon

NEW BRUNSWICK

    The University of New Brunswick, Fredericton
    Université St. Joseph, Moncton
    Mount Allison University, Sackville

NEWFOUNDLAND

    Memorial University, St. John's

NOVA SCOTIA

    Dalhousie University, Halifax
    St. Mary's University, Halifax

ONTARIO
The University of Toronto, Toronto
York University, Toronto
The University of Western Ontario, London
McMaster University, Hamilton
Carleton University, Ottawa
The University of Ottawa, Ottawa

PRINCE EDWARD ISLAND
St. Dunstan's University, Charlottetown

QUEBEC
The University of Montreal, Montreal
McGill University, Montreal
Loyola College, Montreal
Bishop's University, Lennoxville

SASKATCHEWAN
Regina College, Regina

Some university extension departments offer much more intensive non-credit courses which may be given for two hours two or three times a week. These usually last anywhere from thirteen to thirty weeks, and the fees are proportionately higher ($66 to $120). The two most popular methods employed for this type of course are *En France comme si vous y étiez*, produced by Hachette, Paris and *Voix et images de France*, developed by the École Normale Supérieure de Saint-Cloud.

Many readers will be familiar with *En France comme si vous y étiez*, which was televised over part of the CBC network in 1963–64. A basic text which deals with twenty-six different real-life situations in France is illustrated by twenty-six half-hour films which provide the student with a vividly dramatic visual and oral experience of the material presented in each lesson. Forty long-playing records perfectly co-ordinated with film and text allow the student unlimited opportunity for personal review and drill. This method is used for some of the courses offered by the Extension Department of the University of Toronto and McMaster University, Hamilton.

The *Voix et images de France* method is being widely used throughout the world, and many Canadian university extension departments have adopted it. It is based on the vocabulary and grammatical structures of an analytical study of French called *Le français fondamental*. The student is expected to learn and make use of 1500 structures and words with which he should be able to express himself correctly in the ordinary activities of daily life. The *Voix et images de France* method is divided into two levels, the *premier degré* (first degree) and *deuxième degré* (second degree). The first level in turn is divided into two sections, Part I and Part II. The first degree is intended for students having little or no knowledge of French. Emphasis is on conversational French, and very often students are required to spend a certain amount of time each week in the university language laboratory. From Part I, students proceed to Part II where the level is higher. The second degree is still more advanced.

Universities which offer the *Voix et images* programme include the following:

ALBERTA
    The University of Alberta, Edmonton
    The University of Alberta, Calgary

BRITISH COLUMBIA
    The University of British Columbia, Vancouver

NEW BRUNSWICK
    Université St. Joseph, Moncton

NOVA SCOTIA
   Dalhousie University, Halifax

ONTARIO
   York University, Toronto

QUEBEC
   The University of Montreal, Montreal

At the present time the *Voix et images* programme is being revised for use in Canada by a special committee headed by Professor Jean-Paul Vinay of the University of Montreal, himself a television performer known to thousands of viewers in the East especially.

# Summer Schools

MANY CANADIAN UNIVERSITIES operate summer sessions during July and/or August. Like regular fall and winter courses, their offerings may be divided into credit courses (mainly for school teachers wishing to improve their academic qualifications) and non-credit courses. In general, individual classes are given two hours a day, five days a week.

As far as language learning is concerned, a summer session programme is not the ideal method. Spaced learning is more effective than intensive concentration over a relatively brief period where the fluency acquired tends to disappear just as quickly unless protective measures are taken. This is particularly true of French when taught in English-speaking communities, and that is no doubt why some universities have set up summer schools in French-speaking areas. Here the student is exposed to the language all day and he can practise in real-life situations the lessons which he has learned in class.

The Banff Summer School of Fine Arts offers a six-week non-credit course in oral French which consists of twenty hours of instruction per week at a total fee of $85. There are French residences where students are pledged to use French only in order to try and counteract the influence of an English atmosphere. Banff offers many attractions to tourists and the School of Fine Arts has an international reputation because of its work in music, painting, acting, ballet, creative writing, etc. Its French instructors are always highly competent, but there are many distractions that might be allowed to hinder serious language study.

Since 1933 the University of Western Ontario in London has operated a French summer school at Trois Pistoles, Quebec. The term normally runs from July 2 to mid-August, and courses are open to anyone over eighteen years of age. Tuition amounts to $75, and students are housed with French-Canadian families. Class groups are kept small and instructors are under the direction of Professor T. J. Casaubon of the University of Western Ontario.

The University of Toronto recently established a summer school for oral French on the islands of Saint-Pierre and Miquelon, twelve miles off the coast of New-foundland. These islands are France's oldest overseas settlements, and even though 2,000 miles of the Atlantic separate them from the Motherland, their 5,000 in-habitants, mainly from families in the Basque country and in Brittany and Normandy, have maintained the traditions of these old French provinces. Tuition is about $100 for 4 weeks (July or August), and students are housed with families as far as possible. The major item of expense, of course, is transportation. Saint-Pierre and Miquelon are reached by airplane from Sydney, Nova Scotia ($40 return). Founder and director of the school is Professor C. R. Parsons of the University of Toronto.

The University of Montreal has provided summer instruction in oral French at a variety of levels since 1945. Classes are given three hours a day for six weeks, and fees total $200. Students are mostly accommodated in

university residences. Montreal is the second largest
French-speaking city in the world (second only to Paris),
and it offers a great deal to its visitors, especially to those
who wish to live in a French atmosphere while still
enjoying the amenities of North American comfort.

One should mention the summer programmes in
French offered currently at Brandon College, Brandon,
Manitoba, the University of British Columbia in Vancouver, the University of New Brunswick in Fredericton,
as well as those of numerous American institutions, the
best known of which is probably Middlebury, in Ver-
mont. Information about courses and fees may be
obtained on inquiry to the institution concerned.

# The Language Laboratory

THE CONCEPT of a language "laboratory" is startling on first consideration. The application of scientific techniques to the teaching of language, with all the associated ideas of mass education and standardization, seems incompatible with the accepted notion of desirable procedures in language study. But it should be remembered that similar arguments were advanced against chemistry and physics laboratories at a time when these subjects were mainly theoretical. If any demonstration were needed, the teacher would provide it, just as many teachers in language classes still do most of the talking, with the result that students get little if any opportunity to practise. The language laboratory is designed to give all students systematic practice in acquiring the essential oral-aural skills of a language.

The first university language laboratories were set up at Cornell University about thirty years ago, and they were soon imitated by other universities, especially during the war years when it became essential to train very quickly large numbers of servicemen in many European and Eastern languages, some of which were quite unknown in the United States. The successful techniques evolved from these experiments on vast numbers of students have been incorporated into modern college and university language laboratories, whose importance and value have been widely accepted in language schools on this continent.

It is interesting to note in passing that the language departments at Cornell University, the pioneer in this field, have discovered that best results in language teaching are obtained when work in the language laboratory is complemented by tutorials with "native" speakers appointed to coach students individually or in groups. These tutors work closely with lecturers in the language, and they might be regarded as personalized, more efficient, and higher-priced laboratories.

The adult student learning French will probably be introduced to the language laboratory if he takes extension courses at a university or collegiate institute. The laboratory might be a very elaborate one with a large room surveyed by a glassed-in control booth, or it might be a relatively simple one with a limited number of desk-units connected with a master-panel controlled by the instructor.

Basically, each desk-unit consists of a set of earphones through which the student hears French records or tapes, and a microphone for reproducing or recording his own voice. He may play the records or tapes himself, or they may be played at the central control unit. Similarly, he may record his own voice on wax discs or magnetic tape, interspersing spoken passages on the records with his own imitations of them for later listening and criticism.

It would be tedious to try to describe all the technical refinements of the many different systems of electronic laboratories to be found in schools and universities across the country. If you are fortunate enough to be able to enroll in a French course where such equipment is available, the instructor in charge will soon initiate you into the mysteries of the particular type which he is using.

If you are in a smaller centre, or if you are trying to learn French entirely on your own, you might well consider setting up your own language laboratory. All you need is a record player and a tape-recorder. Many of the language records currently available consist mainly of spoken phrases followed by a pause during which the listener repeats what he has just heard. After practising such an exercise several times, it is most useful to record on tape both the original record and the interspersed imitations. When one listens to one's own voice in this way, the assessment is quite impartial and many features can be noticed which mere repetition does not bring to the attention.

It is perfectly true that we never hear ourselves as others do, and listening to a recording of one's own voice in English can be just as humbling an experience as hearing one's inadequate efforts in French. The value of a recording lies in the detachment of the listener. He notices his mistakes and sets out to correct them. This process can be speeded up and performed more efficiently if he has the help of a skilled teacher, but even when working entirely on his own tremendous progress can be made. The cost of equipment is not as high as might be imagined. Tapes can be used over and over again, and once a suitable machine has been purchased, upkeep is negligible if the machine is treated with the proper care.

There are many types of tape-recorders on the market, ranging in price all the way from $30 or $40 for a small machine (often of Japanese make) to $1500 or $2000 for the highest quality of stereophonic equipment. It is usually better not to buy the cheapest type of tape-recorder, because the reproduction of the sound is not good enough to be helpful. An adequate machine will probably cost in the neighbourhood of $180 to $200, but it will be found to have many unsuspected uses—recording interesting radio programmes, providing a verbatim transcript of speeches, meetings, family parties, and the like.

It would be difficult to recommend a particular make of tape-recorder. Perhaps the best idea is to visit stores which stock such equipment and to compare qualities and values. Well-known makes in the medium price-range are the Cypher 1 (produced by Intermark) and the Grundig. More expensive brands are available through Ampex, Seabreeze, Telefunken, and other firms. The range is unlimited, and it would be wise to consult your local electronic equipment serviceman. Dealing with all makes of recorders, he is in a good position to tell you which ones stand up to prolonged use and which ones are most easily repaired if anything goes wrong.

# *Dictionaries*

SOONER OR LATER the language learner must purchase a reliable dictionary. This may be a slim volume of indispensable words and phrases which the traveller in Quebec or France will want to tuck into pocket or purse, or it may be a more substantial reference work which will serve for continuing serious study. In any case, it is most important that the dictionary be accurate and up to date. Too many volumes on the market merely propagate archaic expressions or give a word without any indication as to how it is used. Many dictionaries have been compiled in haste by fallible human beings and a poor one is really worse than none at all.

Until one has a good working knowledge of a language it is necessary, of course, to refer to a bilingual dictionary despite certain obvious hazards that are involved. To begin with, it is often quite impossible to give in one language a word that is the exact equivalent of a word in the other language. Abstract ideas are particularly difficult to convey in another language, but even relatively simple concepts may present problems which the uninitiated cannot appreciate. For example, anyone who has studied a second language knows just how disconcerting it is to be asked point blank: How do you say "check-out counter" (or some other typically North American term) in French? There is no pat answer, but the result is that the questioner is liable to go away with the impression that the so-called expert does not know the other language as well as he professed. Here a reliable dictionary can often be of inestimable help both to the beginner and the more advanced student. In the past twenty years many new words have been introduced into French and only a recent dictionary will give the correct translation for such expressions as "nuclear fission," "chain reaction," "astronaut," "space travel," "ball-point pen," and a host of others.

Words which have identical spelling in French and English are always troublesome. These are sometimes called "false friends" because one has the impression that one knows the word and that it is quite unnecessary to look it up in the dictionary. In point of fact, the meaning often is quite different in the two languages, and on occasion much embarrassment can result.

Any Canadian who has travelled in England knows the dangers of certain expressions which have entirely different connotations over there. If an Englishman were to say, "His wife is very homely," for instance, this would not be a reflection on the woman's appearance but rather a tribute to her qualities as a relaxed and friendly hostess.

The same thing is true of many words which have similar orthography in French and English. *Il est très sensible*, for example, does not mean "He is very sensible," but rather "He is very sensitive"—a quite different notion! It is also true, of course, that certain French words are used differently in Quebec and France, but this is a problem we shall come back to in a moment.

Another question of concern to the purchaser of a dictionary is the use of slang (*argot*). We all know that standard English dictionaries make no attempt to keep up with current slang, which tends to change very rapidly, and this is also true of bilingual dictionaries. At the same time, most such dictionaries omit the less transitory language of the streets—the vulgarities and even obscenities which almost everyone knows but no one uses in polite company. It is disconcerting not to be able to discover the meaning of such words in a dictionary which has been expurgated, presumably to protect young readers. The result of the general confusion is that some unsuspecting travellers are unable to distinguish between colloquial and vulgar expressions, and they pick up a colourful vocabulary which they use indiscriminately under the impression that they are using the very latest slang expressions. And it should be noted in this regard that French is much less prudish than English. It is only recently that indecent four-letter words of Anglo-Saxon origin have been set in print in other than strictly pornographic books, but they are still not in "decent" use. Some of their French counterparts, on the other hand, have been so attenuated in meaning that they are commonly used without any conscious trace of their original meaning. This is not to say that they can be used under any circumstances, and the only reliable guide is a dictionary which makes clear the distinction.

There is, to be sure, a basic and relatively stable core vocabulary in French as in English, and the first aim in learning a second language should be to master this element. The best dictionary is one of reasonable size and price in which are included standard expressions, the commonest expressions (whether vulgar or not), new words, and other words likely to prove troublesome.

At the moment, dictionaries on the market which

satisfy these requirements in varying degrees include:

Cassell's *New French–English English–French Dictionary, Canadian Edition* (1962)

Harrap's *Shorter French and English Dictionary*, edited by J. E. Mansion (1947, reprinted a number of times)

Larousse, *Dictionnaire moderne français–anglais/anglais–français* (1960)

These volumes should be available in appropriate bookstores at prices around six or seven dollars.

It has already been mentioned that French-Canadian usage sometimes differs from standard French just as English-Canadian usage differs from British and, to a lesser extent, American usage. Recently the first distinctively Canadian bilingual dictionary has been published, and this would be a useful supplement to one of the above dictionaries:

McClelland and Stewart, *Dictionnaire Canadien Français–Anglais/Anglais–Français* (1962)

After the language learner has acquired a modest working vocabulary he ought to buy a dictionary in the second language. This will have the merit of further increasing his vocabulary while giving him authentic definitions conceived and expressed in French. A universal standard dictionary used throughout the French-speaking world is the

*Petit Larousse*, dictionnaire encyclopédique pour tous (1959)

The price, again, should be around $7. In addition to word definitions, this dictionary also incorporates in a separate section a concise encyclopedia, the whole copiously illustrated. In the *Petit Larousse* there are scores of maps, diagrams, charts, and attractive illustrations which make the book a useful compendium of French culture in general.

# Grammars

GRAMMARS are much like dictionaries in that they fail to keep up with current usage, and many of them pass on archaic rules which contemporary speech does not heed. In English one has only to think of the restrictions about the use of "shall" and "will" or the proper personal pronoun to use after the verb "to be" to realize that a foreigner learning our language would need a better guide than a mere textbook.

This is also true of French, where the conservative influence of traditional grammar is often in direct conflict with popular speech. French teachers and parents, like their English counterparts, are constantly correcting youngsters who persist in following speech patterns which are not yet acceptable. Ultimately some of these forms will enter the language, but pedagogues are slow to give in and most grammars are at least twenty years out of date.

French has a dubious advantage over English, since the French Academy is considered to be the final authority in matters of language. This self-perpetuating body founded by Richelieu in 1635 consists of forty of the most prominent men of letters in France. Among other duties, they are charged with surveillance of the French language. Over the centuries they have published official dictionaries and grammars and at various times they have made pronouncements on questions of usage. Their decisions have not always been approved or even followed, but they do constitute a board of reference which English lacks.

The basic problem with grammar is, of course, that language comes first and the rules are secondary. They are, in fact, nothing more than a codified analysis of the principles which seem to be at work. This is why one so often has to speak of "exceptions to the rule," a concept which can be quite misleading, since the so-called rules are completely artificial things.

In order to analyse language, it is necessary to use grammatical terms invented for the purpose. This highly technical language is useful to the specialist but it may only get in the way of the amateur. It is quite possible to speak a language without knowing any grammar at all, just as it is possible to sing without any knowledge of intervals, harmony, or voice production. The child who learns his mother tongue in the normal way is not concerned about tense, mood, or agreement of verbs and, in fact, he has no need to distinguish between the verb and other parts of speech.

The same is not quite true for an adult learning a second language, particularly if he has been exposed to the discipline of linguistic analysis in his own language. He wants to know how a word is spelled, how its plural is formed, what restrictions govern its use, and so forth.

For this reason, the adult language-learner soon feels the need of a reliable reference grammar in which he can look up necessary information. Such a grammar ought to be fairly substantial, well-indexed, with copious examples chosen from real situations. Far too many grammars illustrate rules with artificially invented sentences which would never be heard anywhere.

To begin with, of course, the reference grammar must be bilingual. French terminology is not the same as English, and for that reason most grammars tend to use English terms so as not to confuse the beginner. Only at a very advanced level is it useful to study closely a grammar written in French for Frenchmen.

All bilingual grammars have their advantages and disadvantages, and it would be very difficult indeed to get unanimity of opinion about them. In the list which follows, no attempt has been made to list the dozens of good texts based on the grammatical approach and designed to be used with an instructor in classes at various levels. Instead, only reference grammars are included—those which give rules and examples under specific headings without exercises or any attempt to progress from simple elements to more complex ones:

H. Ferrar, *A French Reference Grammar* (Oxford University Press, 1955)

Fraser, Squair and Parker, *French Reference Grammar* (Copp Clark, 1942, reprinted 1961)

J. E. Mansion, *French Reference Grammar for Schools and Colleges* (D. C. Heath and Company, n.d.)

After the student has acquired a reasonably good vocabulary in French the most useful reference work is:

Maurice Grevisse, *Le Bon Usage, Grammaire française avec des remarques sur la langue d'aujourd'hui* (Editions J. Duculot, Gembloux, Belgique)

This admirable volume which is constantly being updated includes thousands of examples chosen from the very best contemporary writers and organized under grammatical headings. One of its most interesting features is the conflicting evidence presented by the quotations chosen, many of them breaking all the so-called "rules" quite flagrantly. The study of such a book is salutary after the student has learned the basic principles, but it can only produce confusion and uncertainty if consulted too soon. It is a common axiom in almost every art that you must first know the rules before you are free to break them.

# Libraries

AFTER ONE HAS ACQUIRED a basic knowledge of grammar and a working vocabulary, there is no better way to build on it than to read French books. Novels, detective stories (if you like them), short stories—all of these will provide countless examples of current usage. Moreover, the variety of subject matter is bound to be more complex and more interesting than that of any text or course.

Most public libraries now have some French books on their shelves, or if they do not, they are usually willing to order some if there is any demand for them by interested readers. Some larger cities, like Toronto, have a special branch which has important collections in a variety of languages other than English.

University libraries by their very nature have large collections of French books which usually include works of fiction as well as grammars, volumes of literary criticism, and the standard classics. Generally speaking, university libraries are willing to allow readers in their own communities to use such books if they are not available in the public library.

For those who live in centres where library facilities are limited or non-existent, there are other possibilities. The National Library in Ottawa has a very large and important collection of French books. These are not available directly to borrowers but they may be loaned to other libraries on request. Readers who wish to borrow specific titles may ask their local librarian to procure the book through Ottawa on inter-library loan.

In most provinces there is also a provincial library service connected with the Department of Education or the Extension Department of the provincial university. Such libraries are designed to loan books by mail to readers who have no other sources at their disposal. A letter of inquiry to the regional Department of Education should provide the required information.

It would be impossible to list a bibliography here because of the literally thousands of suggestions that might be included. There are many fine French-Canadian writers as well as a multitude of authors in France whose works are eagerly read in this country by all Francophones.

# Newspapers

THERE IS MUCH to be said in favour of subscribing to a French-language newspaper. A newspaper subscription means that new reading material is entering the home at regular intervals. The subject-matter is usually familiar, at least in part, and the range of topics offers great variety —all the way from editorials and leading articles to current events, sports news, and even comics.

There are inherent dangers here, too, for the literary level of the average newspaper is not very high, and one risks picking up expressions that are not acceptable in cultivated society. At the present time there is a very strong general reaction against anglicisms which are especially in vogue in newspapers (sports, popular music, films, and so forth). The beginner should be careful which newspaper he chooses.

There are many French-language dailies in Quebec, along with *L'Evangeline* in Moncton and *Le Droit* in Ottawa. Probably the best known French-Canadian newspaper is *Le Devoir* in Montreal. There are also some weekly papers, mostly published in Montreal and mostly of the tabloid variety.

It is very informative to read a local French newspaper where this is possible, but English-speaking Canadians in general would have a much better idea of the French-Canadian point of view if they would only take the trouble to read one of the more influential Quebec news-papers. If it is felt that a daily paper would be too time-consuming, it is always possible to subscribe to the Satur-day edition only.

The following are suggestions for consideration:

*Le Devoir*, Montréal (434, rue Notre Dame)
    Annual subscription, $16; Saturday only, $5
*Le Droit*, Ottawa (375 Rideau Street)
    Annual subscription, $17; Saturday only, $5.50
*La Presse*, Montréal (7 James St. West)
    Annual subscription, $18; Saturday only, $6
*Le Soleil*, Quebec (590, rue de la Couronne)
    Annual subscription, $17.50

Among regional French newspapers one might men-tion the following which appear weekly:

ALBERTA: *La Survivance* (Edmonton)
MANITOBA: *La Liberté et le Patriote* (St. Boniface)
ONTARIO: *L'Étoile de Cornwall* (Cornwall)
        *Le Carillon* (Hawkesbury)
        *Le Moniteur* (Hawkesbury)
        *La Revue ontarienne* (London)
        *L'Ami du peuple* (Sudbury)
NEW BRUNSWICK: *L'Aviron* (Campbellton)
               *Le Madawaska* (Edmunston)
NOVA SCOTIA: *Le Petit Courier* (West Pubnico)
SASKATCHEWAN: *L'Étoile* (Gravelbourg)

In addition to French-Canadian newspapers, there are, of course, many newspapers published in France which are widely read in this country. Some of them have special airmail editions, and these are usually available at newspaper stands in hotels, especially in the bigger cities.

The most significant are the following:

*Le Monde*, Paris (5, rue des Italiens, Paris 9)
Weekly airmail edition (subscription only), 30 francs 50 centimes per year

*Le Figaro littéraire*, Paris (14, Rond-Point des Champs-Élysées, Paris 8)
Weekly at about 40 cents per issue

In addition one might mention a special publication directed toward those interested in French living on this continent. It contains news of France along with items connected with French culture in the United States and Canada touring theatre companies, opera, ballet, art, sports, lectures, etc.).

*France–Amérique*, New York (1111 Lexington Avenue, New York 21)
Annual subscription, $7; Special student rate, $5

# Magazines and Periodicals

THERE ARE LITERALLY HUNDREDS of French-language periodicals available, ranging all the way from specialized learned journals to the most blatant tabloids. As in the case of books, the best way to find what you want is to browse around in shops which have a large selection. Visits to Montreal or other large cities which have French bookstores can be helpful in this regard, since tastes in reading vary so greatly. Where this is not possible, one can always write to a publisher for a few sample copies of magazines before subscribing. They are usually very willing to send recent back issues on request.

In Canada both *Maclean's Magazine* and *Chatelaine* initiated French editions a few years ago. These are not just translations of the English edition, although a few important articles do appear in both. The French edition has its own editorial staff and it reflects in its pages the views of responsible French Canadians on a great many of the important issues of the day. These magazines come out once a month and at $1 or $2 per year, they are bargains. The address for subscriptions is Service du Tirage, *Le Magazine Maclean*, or *Chatelaine, la Revue moderne*, both at 2055, rue Peel, Montréal 2.

Another favourite magazine which appears in a French edition is the *Reader's Digest*. Actually, there are two separate French editions, one published in Paris and the other in Montreal. Opinions about the *Reader's Digest* are often strongly partisan, but the selections always offer great variety and the French edition (*Sélections du Reader's Digest*) can be very helpful to the language student in that the subject matter may be partly familiar from having appeared elsewhere in English. An annual subscription, costing $2.97, may be had by writing to The Reader's Digest Association, 215 Redfern Avenue, Montreal 6.

Among magazines published in French, the best known is undoubtedly *Paris-Match*. It appears weekly and is a sort of combination *Life* and *Time* with feature articles, editorials, and current news. It is superbly illustrated and is read widely throughout France and all the rest of the French-speaking world. An annual subscription costs $16 and may be placed with Hachette, 425, rue Guy, Montreal.

Another weekly publication of interest is *L'Express*. It mainly contains articles on literature, politics, and current events and is much less profusely illustrated than *Paris-Match*. The annual subscription rate is 90 N.F. (about $18). The address is 25, rue de Berri, Paris.

*Elle* is a monthly magazine dealing with women's life in France. It contains the latest news on fashions but also includes more general articles. It is extensively illustrated, and the annual subscription rate is $20.

*Plaisir de France* is France's most beautiful magazine. Each month it offers articles on the Arts, Decoration, Architecture, Travel, History and Science, Fashion, Theatre, and the like. There are three special issues: the Spring number on travel, the June edition on country homes, and the superb Christmas issue on Art. The annual subscription is $19.

Readers with special interests will most likely find that there is a French periodical available in the field. For information concerning the many hundreds of specialized periodicals published regularly in France one may write to

> L'Union Nationale des Éditeurs-Exportateurs
>     de Publications Françaises
> 55, avenue des Champs-Elysées
> Paris 8, France

For similar information concerning French-Canadian periodicals, the corresponding address is

> L'Association Canadienne Française de Périodiques
> 3495, avenue de la Montagne
> Suite 11
> Montréal, P.Q.

Periodicals of rather general interest published in Canada include the following:

> *Actualité*
> 4209, rue de Bordeaux
> Montréal 34, P.Q.
>
> *Mon Mariage*
> 5165 ouest, rue Sherbrooke
> Montréal, P.Q.
>
> *Radiomonde et Télémonde*
> 8430, rue Casgrain
> Montréal, P.Q.
>
> *Relations*
> 8100, boulevard St-Laurent
> Montréal, P.Q.

*La Voix Nationale*
3502, rue Hutchison
Montréal, P.Q.

More specialized titles which will offer current reading material of interest to teachers, businessmen, and persons in various types of professions will be found among the following:

*L'Action médicale*
1450, rue Beaudry
Montréal, P.Q.

*Les Affaires*
635 est, rue Henri-Bourassa
Montréal, P.Q.

*L'Aviculteur québecois*
1273, Chambly
Ste-Foy, P.Q.

*Béton du Québec*
3305, rue Masson
Montréal, P.Q.

*Le Bijoutier*
1448, rue Beaudry
Montréal, P.Q.

*Le Bulletin des agriculteurs*
5670, rue Chauveau
Montréal 5, P.Q.

*Les Cahiers du Nursing canadien*
3745, Chemin Reine-Marie
Montréal 26, P.Q.

*Coiffure et Beauté*
79, rue Ste-Anne
Québec 4, P.Q.

*Collège et Famille*
8100, boulevard St-Laurent
Montréal, P.Q.

*Commerce*
14 est, rue St-Jacques
Montréal, P.Q.

*L'Enseignement*
6330, rue Iberville
Montréal, P.Q.

*La Ferme*
909 est, avenue Mount Royal
Montréal, P.Q.

*Forêt-Conservation*
915 ouest, rue St-Cyrille
Québec, P.Q.

*L'Hôpital d'aujourd'hui*
4370, boulevard Pie IX
Montréal 36, P.Q.

*Information médicale et paramédicale*
3305, rue Masson
Montréal 36, P.Q.

*L'ingénieur*
2500, avenue Guyard
Montréal 29, P.Q.

*Jeune Commerce*
2745, rue Masson
Montréal, P.Q.

*La Loupe*
2950, rue Masson
Montréal, P.Q.

*Le Maître-Électricien*
4073, rue St-Hubert
Montréal, P.Q.

*Le Maître-Imprimeur*
1459 est, rue Bélanger
Montréal, P.Q.

*Le Pêcheur canadien*
160B, rue St-Germain
Rimouski, P.Q.

*Le Photographe professionnel*
Salle 80
1290, rue St. Denis
Montréal 18, P.Q.

*Prestige*
Boîte Postale 8
St-Lambert
Montréal 23, P.Q.

*Le Professionnel*
3305, rue Masson
Montréal 36, P.Q.

*Les Publications financières Inc.*
C.P. 1144
Place d'Armes
Montréal, P.Q.

*Québec-industriel*
4180, avenue de Courtrai
Bureau 300
Montréal, P.Q.

*La Revue du Notariat*
4840, avenue O'Bryan
Montréal 29, P.Q.

*La Revue des Pharmacies*
Carré Phillips
Montréal 2, P.Q.

*La Revue scolaire*
251 est, rue Vitré
Montréal, P.Q.

*Transport routier du Québec*
5165 ouest, rue Sherbrooke
Montréal, P.Q.

*Le Travail* (Labour Magazine)
1001, rue St. Denis
Montréal 18, P.Q.

*L'Union médicale du Canada*
5064, avenue du Parc
Montréal 8, P.Q.

*Vie étudiante*
3305, rue Masson
Montréal, P.Q.

*Les Vivres*
4180, avenue de Courtrai
Bureau 300
Montréal, P.Q.

# *Bookstores*

NOT THE LEAST DIFFICULT PROBLEM connected with the desire to purchase French newspapers, magazines, and books is the scarcity of bookstores handling such material. Outside of the province of Quebec, there are few stores which regularly stock publications in French. It is always possible to ask a local bookseller to order a specific title, although the mark-up is likely to be high, but the delay and the risk of not getting exactly what you want sometimes takes away much of the pleasure. Part of the joy of discovery is to be found in browsing among French books both new and second-hand.

A few of the larger English-speaking Canadian cities have specialized bookstores where works in French may be found. Very often university bookstores carry a sampling of more than just prescribed textbooks. If you are interested, the best idea is to consult the yellow pages in your telephone directory and try to locate a bookstore which has French books in stock.

For those who live in smaller centres, the only alternative is to order by mail. This may be done directly from France, but it is probably simpler to use a Montreal agent in order to avoid complications with customs, bank exchange, and so forth. The cost will not likely be any higher, and most French publishers have representatives in Montreal.

As a start, one might ask for sample catalogues in a particular field (fiction, records, language texts). An order for a dictionary or a reference grammar could be placed with the agent to indicate genuine interest. The most important point to remember is that a bookseller will not continue to send you catalogues and other publicity unless you place orders with him from time to time. Once you have established friendly relations, you will probably find such a mail-order system perfectly satisfactory.

It would be difficult to list even a fraction of the reputable booksellers in Montreal. The following list includes several of the largest whose operations are so extensive that they have most common works in stock or can easily get them. They are also more willing to take back in exchange books that are unsatisfactory for one reason or another, and their prices, of necessity, are always competitive.

Centre Éducatif et Culturel
190, Sauvé Ouest
Montréal 12, P.Q.

Fomac Ltée
480, rue de Lagauchetière ouest
Montréal 1, P.Q.

Librairie Flammarion
1029 Beaver Hall Hill
Montréal, P.Q.

Librairie Hachette
914, rue St. Denis
Montréal, P.Q.

For general information on French-Canadian publishers and booksellers, readers might write to:

> L'Association des Éditeurs Canadiens
> Secrétariat
> 3405, rue St. Denis
> Montréal 18, P.Q.

It would be impossible to list even all the large bookstores in Quebec which publish and sell French-Canadian books. Many specialize in certain types of publications but all will gladly send out catalogues and announcements of forthcoming items.

The following list includes a selection of well-known Montreal firms:

> La Centrale du livre
> 260 ouest, rue Faillon
> Montréal 10, P.Q.

> Les Éditions du jour
> 3411, rue St. Denis
> Montréal 18, P.Q.

> Librairie Beauchemin
> 450, avenue Beaumont
> Montréal 15, P.Q.

> Librairie Déom
> 1247, rue St. Denis
> Montréal 18, P.Q.

> Librairie Dussault
> 1315, rue Lafontaine
> Montréal, P.Q.

> Librairie Fidès
> 245 est, boulevard Dorchester
> Montréal, P.Q.

Librairie Universelle
5165, Côte des Neiges
Montréal, P.Q.

There are many American bookstores which specialize in French books, but again one encounters the problems of customs, duty, and the like. The following, however, issue important catalogues, and on occasion it may be worth while to send for items not available elsewhere:

French and European Publications, Inc.
Librairie de France, Inc.
Rockefeller Center, French Building
610 Fifth Avenue
New York, N.Y. 10020

Goldsmith's Bookstore
401 West 42nd Street
New York 36, N.Y.

Wible Language Institute
24 South 8th Street
Allentown, Penn. 18105

# *Book Clubs*

IN BOTH FRANCE AND QUEBEC there are many book clubs similar in concept to the Book-of-the-Month Club. Sometimes participants are free to choose selections from a current list and sometimes they must agree to accept the club's choice. The number of books also varies from three or four to twelve per year, with some clubs concentrating on the latest fiction and others on beautifully bound and illustrated volumes. On the whole, the relative expense is fairly low, since most French books appear in paper jackets with uncut pages. Students who have acquired sufficient knowledge of the language to be interested in receiving books regularly should write for complete information to one of the following groups. In some cases, they may be referred to a Canadian representative:

> Club du livre
> 90 bis, rue Breteuil
> Marseille 6, France

> Club du livre du mois
> 25, rue Louis-le-Grand
> Paris 2, France

> Club du livre selectionné
> 6, rue de Londres
> Paris 9, France

Club du meilleur livre
3, rue de Grenelle
Paris 6, France

Club français du livre
8, rue de la Paix
Paris, France

La Guilde du livre
4, avenue de la Gare
Lausanne, Switzerland

The best-known book club in Quebec is the

Cercle du livre de France
3300, boulevard Rosemont
Montréal 36, P.Q.

It includes in its selections French-Canadian fiction and non-fiction as well as books by French authors.

# Songs and Music

IT WOULD BE IMPOSSIBLE to give any sort of recommended listing from among all the thousands of recordings of French songs. In recent years many such recordings intended for educational purposes have been accompanied by a text which includes the lyrics and sometimes also a separate piano part for those able to use it.

Another refinement is the "sing-along" record in French. Here a phrase is sung by the recording artist and then the accompaniment is repeated in order for the listener to imitate the singer. At the end, the whole song is gone over and sometimes a complete accompaniment is also included separately so that the learner may sing the song on his own, presumably in the privacy of his living-room!

Learning French songs is undoubtedly a very effective way to perfect one's accent. Music plays an important part in the life of the average French-speaking person— probably a more important part than it does for those whose native language is English. Folk-songs in particular are known and sung in groups on social occasions by all French Canadians. Most of us are familiar at least with *Alouette*, but there are many other fine characteristic folk-songs both of the repeated stanza type and of the built-up refrain variety which we find in *Alouette*.

Good beginning records are the following:

*Alouette and Bon Homm', Bon Homm'*

Foreign Language Series: French, 15 minutes; Foreign Language Department Audio-Visual Center, University of Connecticut.

Professor Croteau, with students, gives instruction in the pronunciation of the words of two songs. Listeners are invited to repeat the lines and sing selected stanzas, a first time slowly and a second time at the proper lively tempo.

*French Christmas Carols*

Foreign Language Series: French, 15 minutes; Foreign Language Department and Audio-Visual Center, University of Connecticut.

Miss Anne Marie Lair of Paris, France, working under the supervision of Professor Croteau, gives instruction in the pronunciation of the words of 3 Christmas carols. The carols are "Les Anges dans nos campagnes," "Minuit, Chrétiens," "Un Flambeau Jeannette, Isabelle". Listeners are invited by Miss Lair to repeat the words and sing the songs, according to her instructions.

*French Folk-Songs*

Foreign Language Series: French, 15 minutes; Foreign Language Department and Audio-Visual Center, University of Connecticut.

Miss Anne Marie Lair of Paris, France, working under the supervision of Professor Croteau, gives instruction in the pronunciation of the words of three folk-songs. The folk-songs are *Au clair de la lune, Il était une bergère,* and *En passant par la Lorraine.* Listeners are invited by Miss Lair to repeat the words and sing the songs according to her instructions.

*French-Canada Folk-Songs*
 Two 12-inch 33⅓ r.p.m. records.
 PRODUCER: Folkways Records
 DISTRIBUTOR:
>  Allied Record Corporation
>  5963 Monkland Avenue
>  Montreal, P.Q.

The first record includes twenty-five folk-songs recorded by Jacques Labrecque. The second (available separately) includes twenty-five selections with solo and group singing. Artists are Laura Boulton and Sam Gesser. Both records are accompanied by a text with detailed notes and song lyrics in French with English translations. *Price*: $5.95 per record.

*Chantons en Francais*
 Four 12-inch 33⅓ r.p.m. records.
 PRODUCER: Folkways Records
 DISTRIBUTOR:
>  Allied Record Corporation
>  5963 Monkland Avenue
>  Montreal, P.Q.

Songs for learning French are sung by Alan Mills and Hélène Baillargeon. They are available separately or in two boxed sets. A manual for each record includes texts in French and English. *Price*: $4.98 per record.

*Let's Sing Songs in French*
 One 12-inch 33⅓ r.p.m. record with eight songs.
 PRODUCER–DISTRIBUTOR:
>  Ottenheimer Publishers, Inc.
>  99 Painters Mill Road
>  Owings Mills, Maryland, 21117

Lyrics are spoken first, then sung with music, and then the listener is invited to sing with the record. An accompanying manual includes lyrics in both English and French plus piano accompaniment. *Price*: $4.98 per record.

Catalogue guides including many hundreds of recordings are available from the following:

> Goldsmith's Music Shop, Inc.
> 401 West 42nd Street
> New York, N.Y.
>
> Wible Language Institute
> 24 South Eighth Street
> Allentown, Penn. 18105

Canadians may have difficulties with customs if ordering direct, but these catalogues will provide many useful suggestions for items which may be ordered locally.

# Exchange Visits

THERE is a quite well developed programme of summer exchange visits for high-school students which comes under the organization *Visites interprovinciales*, 113 St. George Street, Toronto. Under this plan, pairs of youngsters of the same sex, age, and background spend one month in the home of the French person in Quebec and one month in the English person's home in Ontario or the West. Other variations are possible. The length of time may be shortened or, if preferred, one visit may take place in one year and the exchange the following summer. No direct expense is involved except for spending-money and travel, which of course becomes a more important item the further west one goes. This is probably why the scheme is most popular in the two adjacent provinces of Ontario and Quebec.

*Visites interprovinciales* caters exclusively to high-school students, but it is mentioned here for the benefit of those who may have teen-agers in their home. Interest and incentive are immensely stimulated by the presence in the house of a French-Canadian youngster, and the whole family benefits. Also, the links with a French-Canadian family can help to establish friendships and correspondences which will continue over the years.

It is always possible to invite French-speaking visitors

independently, of course, but sometimes there are risks involved. One wants to be sure, for instance, that they will find a congenial atmosphere and that they will be ready to make the necessary adjustments. Some individuals known to the author of this book have shown great ingenuity in arranging highly successful exchange visits. They have written to the Chamber of Commerce of a French-Canadian town chosen at random, to a local Rotary Club or Board of Education. It takes time and persistence to find the right answer in each case, but the results can be very rewarding for language study and for mutual understanding.

It is even more complicated to sponsor an immigrant from France, but this also can be done. The problem, again, is to find a suitable individual who is willing to come to Canada with all the uncertainties and risks involved. Further information may be obtained from The Canadian Embassy, 35 avenue Montaigne, Paris 8, or the Centre international de la jeunesse, 20, rue Jean-Jacques Rousseau, Paris 1, France.

# International Correspondence

THE NOTION of a "pen-pal" is probably best suited to younger students, since most adults do not have the time or the inclination to undertake correspondence with strangers in a foreign tongue. Most of us are glad enough if we can keep up with the demands of correspondence within the family!

There are exceptions, of course, and for those interested an exchange of letters in French and English can be most stimulating. Sometimes the French writer will try to use English only, while his correspondent uses French, but more often each writer composes a part of each letter in both languages.

There are non-profit organizations which will send you the addresses of French correspondents all over the world. For detailed information, adults may write to The International Friendship League, 40 Mt. Vernon Street, Boston, Massachusetts (Membership fee 50¢).

Another type of correspondence that is less demanding on time and linguistically much more challenging is the exchange of tape recordings. Those interested who have access to a tape recorder are invited to write to The Voicespondence Club, Noel, Virginia (Annual membership fee, $3).

# *Miscellaneous*

IN ADDITION to all the specific ways in which one may seek to be exposed to French language and culture, there are in every community other possible leads which may be followed. The learner anxious to make progress as quickly as possible is going to seek out every opportunity to practise French and to hear it.

The first suggestion to investigate is shopping. The French are particularly discriminating about bread and pastries, and almost any area which has French-speaking inhabitants is likely to have a small French bakery or a *pâtisserie française*. There may also be grocery stores or stalls at the market which cater to a French-speaking clientele.

Most communities which have a French-speaking one must be cautious because a French name does not always mean a French proprietor. Very often, it is only an advertising gimmick intended to persuade the unwary that they will be treated to better-than-ordinary cooking.

Most communities which have a French-speaking population also have churches where the services are conducted in French. These are most likely to be Catholic, but there are also some French Protestant churches in Canada.

There are, of course, many professional people who speak French—doctors, dentists, lawyers, and so forth. You may not wish to carry learning French to the extreme of changing your doctor or your dentist, but it is always worth reading the professional notices in local French newspapers where these exist.

# Index

# CANADIAN UNIVERSITY PAPERBOOKS